LAUREN COLES

DELICIOUS RECIPES FOR
ENJOYING A LOW-CARB DIET

low carb
recipes

This is a Parragon Publishing Book
First published in 2004

Parragon Publishing
Queen Street House
4 Queen Street
Bath BA1 1HE, UK

Created and produced by The Bridgewater Book Company Ltd.

ISBN: 1-40543-161-X

Printed in China

NOTE

*This book uses imperial, metric, and US cup measurements. Follow the same units of
measurement throughout; do not mix imperial and metric. All spoon measurements
are level: teaspoons are assumed to be 5 ml and tablespoons are assumed to be 15 ml.
Unless otherwise stated, milk is assumed to be whole, eggs and individual vegetables
such as potatoes are medium, and pepper is freshly ground black pepper.*

*Ovens should be preheated to the specified temperature. If using a fan-assisted oven,
check the manufacturer's instructions for adjusting the time and temperature.*

*Recipes using raw or very lightly cooked eggs should be avoided by infants, the elderly,
pregnant women, convalescents, and anyone suffering from an illness. Pregnant and
breastfeeding women are advised to avoid eating peanuts and peanut products.*

Contents

Introduction

It is true that a balanced intake of all the food groups—fats, proteins, and carbohydrates—in their appropriate proportions is the ideal that nutritionists encourage us to aim for. However, this begs a number of questions: where we are starting from, how old we are, what kind of lives we lead, whether we are men or women, and even how to estimate "a balanced intake" and

"appropriate proportions." Many of us have let the extra weight creep on and developed bad eating patterns that make us fat, unhappy, and ill. A low-carbohydrate diet is one, very successful, way of tackling these sorts of problems, revitalizing and re-energizing the system and trimming off that spare tire.

What are Carbohydrates?

The name of this food group derives from the chemical elements it contains—carbon, hydrogen, and oxygen—which form compounds such as starch and sugars. When these are eaten, the body breaks them down to release energy. They are found in a wide variety of commonly eaten foods. Grains and cereals, for example, feature in

most daily meals. Potatoes are a starchy staple and legumes, such as peas and beans, are also high in carbohydrates. Many popular snacks are packed with sugars. Carbohydrates are comfort foods, making us feel full and satisfied.

Dietary fiber is a second type of carbohydrate that our bodies can't digest. It helps to regulate the digestive system, but the body cannot break it down to release energy. This kind of carbohydrate is found in wheat bran, fruit, beans, nuts, and leafy green vegetables.

Energy and Body Weight

The body needs energy to function and it obtains this from the food consumed. Even the process of digestion uses up energy. However, the amount of energy you require depends on a number of factors. It is obvious that an Olympic athlete requires more input than a sedentary office worker, but age is also a consideration as the

metabolism begins to slow down from about the age of 30. Body type, including the amount of muscle mass and lean tissue, also affects energy requirements.

Energy is measured as calories, also called kilocalories (kcal) and as kilojoules (kJ). 1 kcal equals about 4 kJ. Many of the calories consumed are used quite quickly for everyday activities, from breathing to walking up the stairs. The energy that is not used is converted by the body to be stored in the muscles or as fat. It is easy to

see that if you consume more calories than you use, the body will build up a store of fat.

The following is a guide to the approximate daily calorie intake required by men and women at different stages in life.

Growing children
Boys and girls—1,800-2,220 calories per day

Adults who exercise/have physical jobs
Men—2,850 calories per day
Women—2,150 calories per day

Adults who don't exercise/have sedentary jobs
Men—2,400 calories per day
Women—2 000 calories per day

Over 50s
Men—2,200 calories per day
Women—1,850 calories per day

Low-Carb Benefits

Carbohydrates are the main source of energy in our diets, with fats second, so if you want to lose weight, reducing their intake is a good way to do it. However, cutting them out all together is neither sensible nor practical, as you will also be cutting out important nutrients. It is also unwise to embark on a drastic reduction of carbohydrates all at once. If you introduce this new eating pattern gradually, you will not encounter the mood swings or hunger pangs that so often go with attempts to diet and usually result in failure.

While it is true that taking in more energy than is expended is the reason why fat accumulates in the body, the individual metabolism also plays a role. Some people are simply more intolerant of carbohydrates than others and can almost see their hips growing with every slice of crispbread. Pay close attention to your body and respond to its particular requirements.

Previously, the most difficult aspect of a low-carbohydrate diet was deciding what to eat, not what to leave out. This is because much of the variety and contrast in our "normal" meals is derived from incorporating carbohydrates. Who wants a steak without fries or meatballs without spaghetti? The problem is now solved because this book provides a wealth of recipes for delicious, low-carbohydrate dishes that are easy to cook and will satisfy the appetite. All the thinking, planning, and calorie counting has been done for you. The recipes, based on meat, poultry, eggs, cheese, and vegetables, offer both variety and enjoyment.

For many people, a low-carbohydrate diet is a lifetime choice, used to maintain their optimum body weight. Others find it a quick way to shed a few pounds before a summer holiday or after an overindulgent Christmas. The choice is, of course, personal, but do bear in mind that if you return to higher carbohydrate meals, you are likely to regain weight.

Ingredients

Labels providing nutritional information on packaged foods are not always as clear and helpful as they might be. However, carbohydrate content is normally included and covers both starches and sugars. You may find it helpful to know that 1 gram of carbohydrate supplies about 3.75 calories or 16 kilojoules of energy. Dietary fiber—non-digestible carbohydrates—is usually listed separately. Not all products include a measure of fiber, either because there isn't any or because figures are not available.

There is no reason why you shouldn't substitute one ingredient for another in any of these recipes, provided that it does not increase the carbohydrate count. While Brie contains only traces of carbohydrate, Stilton may have 2 grams per 100 grams—a small difference, but it will up the count. Cauliflower contains almost twice as much carbohydrate as broccoli. Also, bear in mind that some most unexpected foods, including accompaniments and drinks, are high in carbohydrates. These will contribute to the overall

N.B. The nutritional analysis given for the recipes in this book does not include optional ingredients or serving suggestions.

count. It's no good cooking a low-carbohydrate curry and serving it with a high-carbohydrate chutney. At the same time, there is no point in being obsessive. English mustard may contain about 19 grams of carbohydrate per 100 ml, but when did you last eat more than ½ teaspoon at one sitting? The desserts contain more carbohydrates than the other recipes in this book, but are low in comparison to most other desserts.

There are some specially manufactured low-carbohydrate products on the market. These are often quite expensive and their labels require close scrutiny. Jellies and spreads produced without added sugar will contain some natural fruit sugars, but are generally a good buy. Low-carbohydrate baked goods may be life-savers for some, but these vary in quality, while sugarfree candies and chocolates, originally produced for diabetes sufferers, have a good reputation.

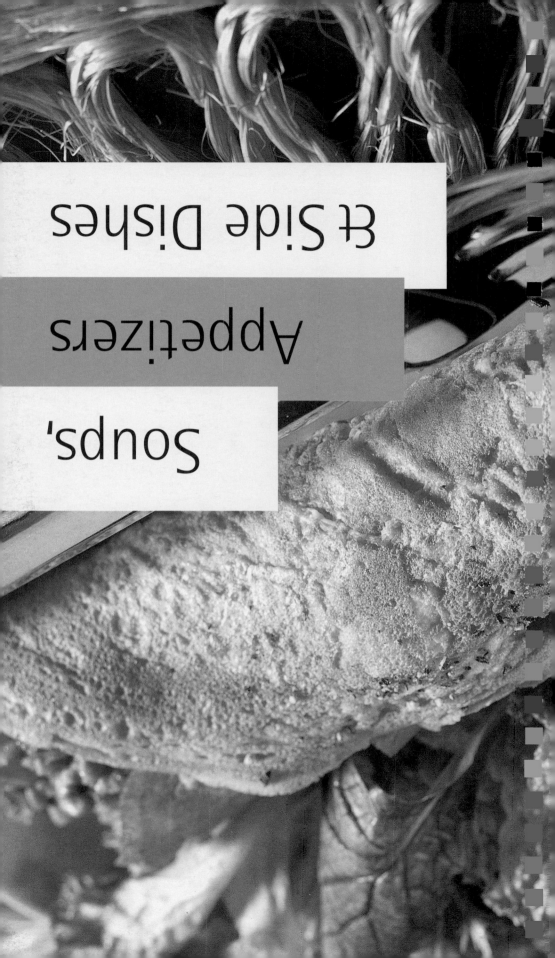

Soups,
Appetizers
& Side Dishes

Cream of Chicken Soup

Tarragon adds a delicate anise flavor to this tasty soup. If you can't find tarragon, use parsley for a fresh taste.

serves 4

½ stick unsalted butter

1 large onion, chopped

10½ oz/300 g cooked chicken, finely shredded

2½ cups chicken stock

salt and pepper

1 tbsp chopped fresh tarragon

⅔ cup heavy cream

Croutons (optional)

4 thick slices day-old bread

4 tbsp olive oil

fresh tarragon leaves, to garnish

Method

❶ Melt the butter in a large, heavy-bottom pan, then add the onion and cook for 3 minutes. Add the chicken to the pan with 1¼ cups of the stock.

❷ Bring to a boil, then let simmer for 20 minutes. Remove the pan from the heat and let cool, then transfer the soup to a food processor or blender and process until smooth.

❸ Add the remainder of the stock and season to taste. Add the tarragon, then pour the soup into a tureen or individual bowls and add a swirl of cream.

❹ If you are making croutons, cut the bread into even-size cubes. Heat the oil in a skillet. Add the bread cubes and cook until golden brown and crisp. Drain on paper towels and set aside until required.

❺ Garnish the soup with fresh tarragon and serve with the croutons.

Nutritional Information

Calories	420	Sugars	4g
Protein	24g	Fat	33g
Carbohydrate	6g	Saturates	20g

Chile & Watercress Soup

This delicious soup is a wonderful blend of colors and flavors. It is very hot, so if you prefer a milder taste, omit the seeds from the chiles.

serves 4

1 tbsp corn oil

9 oz/250 g smoked tofu
(drained weight), sliced

1½ cups sliced shiitake mushrooms

2 tbsp chopped cilantro

4½ oz/125 g watercress or arugula

1 fresh red chile, seeded and finely sliced,
to garnish

Stock

1 tbsp tamarind pulp

2 dried red chiles, chopped

2 kaffir lime leaves, torn in half

1-inch/2.5-cm piece fresh
gingerroot, chopped

2-inch/5-cm piece galangal, chopped

1 lemongrass stem, chopped

1 onion, cut into fourths

4 cups cold water

Method

❶ Place all the ingredients for the stock in a pan and bring to a boil.

❷ Simmer the stock for 5 minutes. Remove from the heat and strain, reserving the stock.

❸ Heat the corn oil in a preheated wok or large, heavy-bottom skillet and cook the tofu over high heat for about 2 minutes, stirring constantly so that the tofu cooks evenly on both sides. Add the strained stock to the skillet.

❹ Add the mushrooms and cilantro and boil for 3 minutes. Add the watercress and boil for an additional 1 minute.

❺ Serve at once, garnished with red chile slices.

Nutritional Information

Calories	90	Sugars	1g
Protein	7g	Fat	6g
Carbohydrate	2g	Saturates	1g

Spinach & Ginger Soup

This mildly spiced, rich green soup is delicately scented with ginger and lemongrass. It makes a good light appetizer or summer lunch dish.

serves 4

2 tbsp corn oil

1 onion, chopped

2 garlic cloves, finely chopped

2 tsp finely chopped fresh gingerroot

generous 5½ cups young spinach leaves

1 small lemongrass stem, finely chopped

4 cups vegetable stock

8 oz/225 g potatoes, chopped

1 tbsp rice wine or dry sherry

salt and pepper

1 tsp sesame oil

Method

❶ Heat the oil in a large pan. Add the onion, garlic, and ginger and cook over low heat, stirring occasionally, for 3–4 minutes, or until softened.

❷ Set aside 2–3 small spinach leaves. Add the remaining leaves and lemongrass to the pan, stirring until the spinach is wilted. Add the stock and potatoes to the pan and bring to a boil. Reduce the heat, then cover the pan and let simmer for about 10 minutes.

❸ Remove the pan from the heat and set aside to cool slightly. Tip the soup into a blender or food processor and process until completely smooth.

❹ Return the soup to the pan and add the rice wine or sherry, then adjust the seasoning to taste with salt and pepper. Heat until just about to boil.

❺ Finely shred the reserved spinach leaves and sprinkle some over the top. Drizzle a few drops of sesame oil into the soup. Ladle into warmed soup bowls and sprinkle the remaining shredded spinach on each, then serve the soup at once.

Nutritional Information

Calories	38	Sugars	0.8g
Protein	3.2g	Fat	1.8g
Carbohydrate	2.4g	Saturates	0.2g

Chinese Crab Soup

Two classic ingredients in Chinese cooking, ginger and soy sauce, are blended together in this recipe for a very special soup. Light soy sauce is used because it will not overpower all the other flavors.

serves 4

1 carrot, chopped

1 leek, chopped

1 bay leaf

3½ cups fish stock

2 medium-size cooked crabs

1-inch/2.5-cm piece fresh gingerroot, grated

1 tsp light soy sauce

½ tsp ground star anise

salt and pepper

Method

❶ Place the carrot, leek, bay leaf, and stock in a large, heavy-bottom pan and bring to a boil over medium heat. Reduce the heat, then cover and let simmer for 10 minutes, or until the vegetables are nearly tender.

❷ Meanwhile, remove the meat from the cooked crabs. Break off the claws and break the joints, then remove the meat (you may need a fork or skewer for this). Add the crabmeat to the stock in the pan.

❸ Add the ginger, soy sauce, and star anise to the stock and bring to a boil. Reduce the heat and let simmer for 10 minutes, or until the vegetables are tender and the crab is heated through. Season to taste with salt and pepper.

❹ Ladle the soup into 4 warmed serving bowls and garnish with crab claws. Serve at once.

Nutritional Information

Calories	145	Sugars	2.4g
Protein	40g	Fat	5.7g
Carbohydrate	2.7g	Saturates	2.6g

Grilled Smoked Salmon

It is best to buy packages of smoked salmon slices for this recipe because they lend themselves to folding more easily than freshly sliced salmon.

serves 4

12 oz/350 g sliced smoked salmon

1 tsp Dijon mustard

1 garlic clove, crushed

2 tsp chopped fresh dill

2 tsp sherry vinegar

4 tbsp olive oil

4 oz/115 g mixed salad greens

salt and pepper

To garnish

fresh dill sprigs

mixed lemon, lime, and orange slices

Method

❶ Fold the slices of smoked salmon, making 2 folds accordion-style, so that they form little packages.

❷ To make the vinaigrette, whisk the mustard, garlic, dill, vinegar, and seasoning together in a small bowl. Gradually whisk in the olive oil to form a light emulsion.

❸ Heat a ridged grill pan over medium heat until smoking. Add the salmon packages and cook on one side only for 2–3 minutes, or until heated through and seared from the pan.

❹ Meanwhile, dress the salad greens with some of the vinaigrette and divide between 4 serving plates. Top with the cooked smoked salmon, cooked side up. Drizzle with the remaining dressing. Serve, garnished with a few sprigs of fresh dill and a mixture of lemon, lime, and orange slices.

Variation

This recipe would also work very well with smoked trout.

Nutritional Information

Calories	115	Sugars	1g
Protein	23g	Fat	15g
Carbohydrate	1g	Saturates	2g

Lettuce-Wrapped Meat

Serve the ground meat and lettuce leaves on separate dishes: each guest then wraps his or her own package.

serves 4

generous 1 cup ground pork or chicken

1 tbsp finely chopped Chinese mushrooms

1 tbsp finely chopped water chestnuts

salt and pepper

pinch of sugar

1 tsp light soy sauce

1 tsp rice wine or dry sherry

1 tsp cornstarch

2–3 tbsp vegetable oil

½ tsp finely chopped fresh gingerroot

1 tsp finely chopped scallions

1 tbsp finely chopped Szechuan preserved vegetables (optional)

1 tbsp oyster sauce

few drops of sesame oil

8 crisp lettuce leaves, to serve

Method

❶ Mix the ground pork with the Chinese mushrooms, water chestnuts, salt, pepper, sugar, soy sauce, rice wine, and cornstarch. Blend well until all the ingredients are thoroughly combined.

❷ Heat the vegetable oil in a preheated wok or large skillet.

❸ Add the ginger and scallions to the wok or skillet, followed by the ground meat. Stir-fry for 1 minute.

❹ Add the preserved vegetables, if using, and continue to stir-fry for 1 minute.

❺ Add the oyster sauce and sesame oil, blend well, and cook for a further 1 minute, or until the juices run clear. Transfer the mixture to a warmed serving dish.

❻ To serve, place about 2–3 tablespoons of the mixture on a lettuce leaf, and roll it up tightly to form a small package. Eat with your fingers.

Nutritional Information

Calories	159	Sugars	0.2g
Protein	14g	Fat	10g
Carbohydrate	1g	Saturates	2g

Eggplant Satay

Eggplants and mushrooms are broiled on skewers and served with a satay sauce.

serves 4

2 eggplants, cut into 1-inch/2.5-cm pieces

6 oz/175 g small cremini mushrooms

Marinade

1 tsp cumin seeds

1 tsp coriander seeds

1-inch/2.5-cm piece fresh
gingerroot, grated

2 garlic cloves, lightly crushed

½ lemongrass stem, coarsely chopped

4 tbsp light soy sauce

8 tbsp corn oil

2 tbsp lemon juice

Peanut sauce

½ tsp cumin seeds

½ tsp coriander seeds

3 garlic cloves

1 small onion, puréed in a food processor
or chopped very finely by hand

1 tbsp lemon juice

1 tsp salt

½ fresh red chile, seeded and sliced

½ cup coconut milk

⅞ cup crunchy peanut butter

1 cup water

Method

❶ Thread the vegetables onto 8 metal or presoaked wooden skewers.

❷ For the marinade, grind the cumin and coriander seeds, ginger, garlic, and lemongrass. Stir-fry over high heat until fragrant. Remove from the heat and add the remaining marinade ingredients. Place the skewers in a dish and spoon the marinade over. Let marinate for at least 2 hours and up to 8 hours.

❸ Preheat the broiler to hot. To make the sauce, grind the cumin and coriander seeds with the garlic. Add all the ingredients except the water. Transfer to a pan and stir in the water. Bring to a boil and cook until thick.

❹ Cook the skewers under the hot broiler for 15–20 minutes. Brush with the marinade frequently and turn once. Serve with the peanut sauce.

Nutritional Information

Calories	155	Sugars	2g
Protein	4g	Fat	14g
Carbohydrate	3g	Saturates	3g

Avocado Cream Terrine

The smooth, rich taste of ripe avocados combines well with thick, creamy yogurt and light cream to make this impressive terrine.

serves 4

2 ripe avocados

4 tbsp cold water

2 tsp gelozone (vegetarian gelatin)

1 tbsp lemon juice

4 tbsp lowfat mayonnaise

$^2/_3$ cup plain yogurt

$^2/_3$ cup light cream

salt and pepper

mixed salad greens, to serve

To garnish

cucumber slices

nasturtium flowers

Method

❶ Peel the avocados and remove and discard the pits. Place the flesh in a blender or food processor or a large bowl with the water, vegetarian gelatin, lemon juice, mayonnaise, yogurt, and cream. Season to taste with salt and pepper.

❷ Process for 10–15 seconds or beat by hand, using a fork or whisk, until smooth.

❸ Transfer the mixture to a small, heavy-bottom pan and heat very gently, stirring constantly, until just starting to boil.

❹ Pour the mixture into a 3½-cup terrine, nonstick loaf pan, or plastic food storage box and smooth the surface. Let the mixture cool and set, then let chill in the refrigerator for 1½–2 hours.

❺ Turn the terrine out of its container and cut into neat slices. Arrange a bed of salad greens on 4 serving plates. Place a slice of avocado terrine on top and garnish with cucumber slices and nasturtium flowers.

Nutritional Information

Calories	327	Sugars	3g
Protein	6g	Fat	32g
Carbohydrate	4g	Saturates	8g

Thai Stuffed Omelet

This makes a substantial appetizer, or a light lunch or supper dish. Serve with a colorful, crisp salad to accompany the dish.

serves 4

2 garlic cloves, chopped

4 black peppercorns

4 cilantro sprigs

2 tbsp vegetable oil

⅞ cup ground pork

2 scallions, chopped

1 large, firm tomato, chopped

6 large eggs

1 tbsp Thai fish sauce

¼ tsp ground turmeric

mixed salad greens, tossed, to serve

Method

❶ Place the garlic, peppercorns, and cilantro in a mortar and, using a pestle, crush to a smooth paste.

❷ Heat 1 tablespoon of the oil in a large skillet over medium heat. Add the paste and stir-fry for 1–2 minutes, or until it just changes color.

❸ Stir in the pork and stir-fry until it is lightly browned. Add the scallions and tomato, and stir-fry for 1 minute, then remove the skillet from the heat.

❹ Heat the remaining oil in a small, heavy-bottom skillet. Beat the eggs with the fish sauce and turmeric, then pour one-quarter of the egg mixture into the skillet. As the mixture starts to set, stir lightly to ensure that all the liquid egg is set.

❺ Spoon one-fourth of the pork mixture down the center of the omelet, then fold the sides inward toward the center, enclosing the filling. Make 3 more omelets with the remaining egg and fill with the remaining pork mixture.

❻ Slide the omelets onto serving plates and serve with salad greens.

Nutritional Information

Calories	250	Sugars	1g
Protein	21g	Fat	18g
Carbohydrate	2g	Saturates	4g

Easy Cauliflower & Broccoli

Whole baby cauliflowers are used in this recipe. Try to find them if you can, but if not use large florets instead.

serves 4

2 baby cauliflowers	**Sauce**
8 oz/225 g broccoli	8 tbsp olive oil
salt and pepper	4 tbsp butter or margarine
	2 tsp grated fresh gingerroot
	juice and rind of 2 lemons
	5 tbsp chopped cilantro
	5 tbsp grated Cheddar cheese

Method

❶ Preheat the broiler. Cut the cauliflowers in half and the broccoli into large florets.

❷ Cook the cauliflower and broccoli in a pan of boiling salted water for 10 minutes. Drain well, then transfer to a shallow ovenproof dish and keep warm until required.

❸ To make the sauce, place the oil and butter in a skillet and heat gently until the butter melts.

❹ Add the ginger, lemon juice, lemon rind, and chopped cilantro and let simmer for 2–3 minutes, stirring occasionally.

❺ Season the sauce with salt and pepper to taste, then pour over the vegetables in the dish and sprinkle the cheese on top.

❻ Cook under the hot broiler for 2–3 minutes, or until the cheese is bubbling and golden brown. Let cool for 1–2 minutes, then serve.

Nutritional Information

Calories	433	Sugars	2g
Protein	8g	Fat	44g
Carbohydrate	3g	Saturates	9g

Roasted Vegetables

Rosemary branches can be used as brushes for basting and as skewers. Soak the rosemary skewers overnight to prevent them charring.

serves 6

1 small red cabbage

1 fennel bulb

1 orange bell pepper, cut into

1½-inch/4-cm dice

1 eggplant, halved and sliced into

½-inch/1-cm pieces

2 zucchini, thickly sliced diagonally

6 rosemary twigs, about 6-inches/15-cm

long, soaked in cold water

olive oil, for brushing

salt and pepper

Method

❶ Preheat the grill or broiler. Place the red cabbage on its side on a cutting board and cut through the middle of its stem and heart. Divide each piece into 4, each time including a section of the stem in the slice to hold it together.

❷ Prepare the fennel in the same way as the red cabbage.

❸ Blanch the red cabbage and fennel in boiling water for 3 minutes, then drain well.

❹ With a wooden skewer, carefully pierce a hole through the center of each piece of vegetable.

❺ Thread a piece of orange bell pepper, fennel, red cabbage, eggplant, and zucchini onto each rosemary twig, gently pushing the rosemary through the skewer holes.

❻ Brush liberally with olive oil and season with plenty of salt and pepper.

❼ Cook over hot coals or under the hot broiler for 8–10 minutes, turning occasionally. Serve at once.

Nutritional Information

Calories	16	Sugars	3g
Protein	1g	Fat	0.3g
Carbohydrate	3g	Saturates	0g

Long Beans with Tomatoes

Indian meals often need some green vegetables to complement the spicy dishes and to offset the richly flavored sauces.

serves 6

1 lb 2 oz/500 g green beans, cut into 2-inch/5-cm lengths

2 tbsp ghee or vegetable oil

1-inch/2.5-cm piece fresh gingerroot, grated

1 garlic clove, crushed

1 tsp ground turmeric

½ tsp cayenne pepper

1 tsp ground coriander

4 tomatoes, peeled, seeded, and diced

⅔ cup vegetable stock

Method

❶ Blanch the beans briefly in boiling water. Drain, then refresh under cold running water and drain again.

❷ Melt the ghee in a preheated wok or large skillet over medium heat. Add the grated ginger and crushed garlic. Stir, then add the turmeric, cayenne, and ground coriander. Stir over low heat for about 1 minute, or until fragrant.

❸ Add the diced tomatoes to the wok, tossing until they are thoroughly coated in the spice mix.

❹ Add the vegetable stock to the wok and bring to a boil, then let simmer over medium–high heat, stirring occasionally, for about 10 minutes, or until the sauce has reduced and thickened.

❺ Add the beans, then reduce the heat to medium and heat through, stirring constantly, for 5 minutes.

❻ Transfer to a warmed serving dish and serve at once.

Nutritional Information

Calories	76	Sugars	3g
Protein	2g	Fat	6g
Carbohydrate	4g	Saturates	3g

Mixed Leaf Salad

Make this green leafy salad with as many varieties of salad greens and edible flowers as you can find to give an unusual effect.

serves 4

½ head frisée	**French dressing**
½ head oak leaf lettuce	1 tbsp white wine vinegar
few leaves of radicchio	pinch of sugar
1 head chicory	½ tsp Dijon mustard
1 oz/25 g arugula leaves	3 tbsp extra virgin olive oil
few fresh basil or flatleaf parsley sprigs	salt and pepper
edible flowers, to garnish (optional)	

Method

❶ Tear the frisée, oak leaf lettuce, and radicchio into pieces. Place the salad greens in a large serving bowl or individual bowls if you prefer.

❷ Cut the chicory into diagonal slices and add to the bowl with the arugula leaves and basil.

❸ To make the dressing, beat the white wine vinegar, sugar, and mustard together in a small bowl until the sugar has dissolved. Gradually beat in the olive oil until the dressing is creamy and thoroughly mixed. Season to taste with salt and pepper.

❹ Pour the dressing over the salad and toss thoroughly. Sprinkle a mixture of edible flowers, if using, over the top, and serve.

Cook's tip

Violas, hardy geraniums, nasturtiums, chive flowers, and pot marigolds add vibrant colors and a sweet flavor to this salad. Use it as a centerpiece at a dinner party, or to liven up a simple everyday meal.

Nutritional Information

Calories	51	Sugars	0.1g
Protein	0.1g	Fat	6g
Carbohydrate	1g	Saturates	1g

Lobster Salad

Lobsters are best prepared simply, to ensure that none of the rich, sweet flavor is lost amid a mass of other ingredients.

serves 4

2 raw lobster tails	**Lemon-dill mayonnaise**
salt and pepper	1 large lemon
	1 large egg yolk
To garnish	½ tsp Dijon mustard
radicchio leaves	⅔ cup olive oil
lemon wedges	1 tbsp chopped fresh dill
fresh dill sprigs	

Method

❶ To make the lemon-dill mayonnaise, finely grate the rind from the lemon and squeeze the juice. Beat the egg yolk in a small bowl and beat in the mustard and 1 teaspoon of the lemon juice.

❷ Using a balloon whisk or electric mixer, beat in the olive oil, drop by drop, until a thick mayonnaise forms. Stir in half the lemon rind and 1 tablespoon of the juice.

❸ Season with salt and pepper, and add more lemon juice if desired. Stir in the dill and cover with plastic wrap. Place in the refrigerator to chill until required.

❹ Bring a large pan of salted water to a boil. Add the lobster tails and continue to cook for 6 minutes, or until the flesh is opaque and the shells are red. Drain at once and let cool completely.

❺ Remove the lobster flesh from the shells and cut into bite-size pieces. Arrange the radicchio leaves on individual plates and top with the lobster flesh. Place a spoonful of the mayonnaise on the side. Garnish with lemon wedges and dill sprigs and serve.

Nutritional Information

Calories	487	Sugars	2g
Protein	24g	Fat	42g
Carbohydrate	2g	Saturates	6g

Green Sesame Salad

A very elegant and light salad which will complement rice and noodle dishes beautifully.

serves 4

scant 1 cup bean sprouts

1½ tbsp chopped cilantro

3 tbsp fresh lime juice

½ tsp mild chili powder

1 tsp sugar

½ tsp salt

3 celery stalks

1 large green bell pepper, seeded

1 large Granny Smith apple

2 tbsp toasted sesame seeds, to garnish

Method

1 Rinse the bean sprouts under cold running water and drain thoroughly.

2 Pick over the bean sprouts, removing any that seem a little brown or limp—it is essential that they are fresh and crunchy for this recipe.

3 To make the dressing, combine the cilantro, lime juice, chili powder, sugar, and salt in a small bowl and mix thoroughly.

4 Using a sharp knife, cut the celery into 1-inch/2.5-cm pieces. Cut the bell pepper into small pieces and the Granny Smith apple into small chunks.

5 Place the chopped celery, bell pepper, apple, and bean sprouts into a large mixing bowl and stir gently to mix.

6 Just before serving, pour the dressing over the salad, tossing well to mix.

7 Garnish the green sesame salad with the toasted sesame seeds and serve with rice or noodle dishes.

Cook's tip

Keeping each ingredient as fresh and crunchy as possible will make all the difference to the appearance and taste of this elegant salad. To prevent the apples going brown, soak the slices briefly in a little lemon juice and water as soon as you have cut them.

Nutritional Information

Calories	78	Sugars	8g
Protein	3g	Fat	3g
Carbohydrate	3g	Saturates	0.5g

Chicory Salad

The contrast of the pink grapefruit, creamy chicory, and bright green corn salad makes this dish look simply stunning.

serves 4

1 pink grapefruit	**French dressing**
1 avocado	3 tbsp olive oil
2 oz/55 g corn salad	1 tbsp wine vinegar
2 heads chicory, sliced diagonally	1 small garlic clove, crushed
1 tbsp chopped fresh mint	½ tsp Dijon or Meaux mustard
	1 tsp honey
	salt and pepper

Method

1 Peel the grapefruit with a serrated knife. Cut the grapefruit into segments by cutting between the membranes. Set aside.

2 To make the French dressing, place the oil, vinegar, garlic, mustard, and honey in a screw-top jar and shake vigorously. Season to taste with salt and pepper. Pour the dressing into a bowl.

3 Halve and pit the avocado and cut it into thin slices. Peel off the skin, then place the sliced flesh in the bowl of French dressing and toss gently to coat.

4 Remove any stems from the corn salad and place in a bowl with the grapefruit, chicory, and chopped mint.

5 Add the avocado slices and 2 tablespoons of the French dressing. Toss well and transfer to individual serving plates. Serve at once.

Cook's tip

Corn salad is also called lamb's lettuce because the shape of its dark green leaves resembles a lamb's tongue. The French call it mâche. It is easy to grow in the garden and will withstand the frost.

Nutritional Information

Calories	137	Sugars	4g
Protein	1g	Fat	13g
Carbohydrate	4g	Saturates	2g

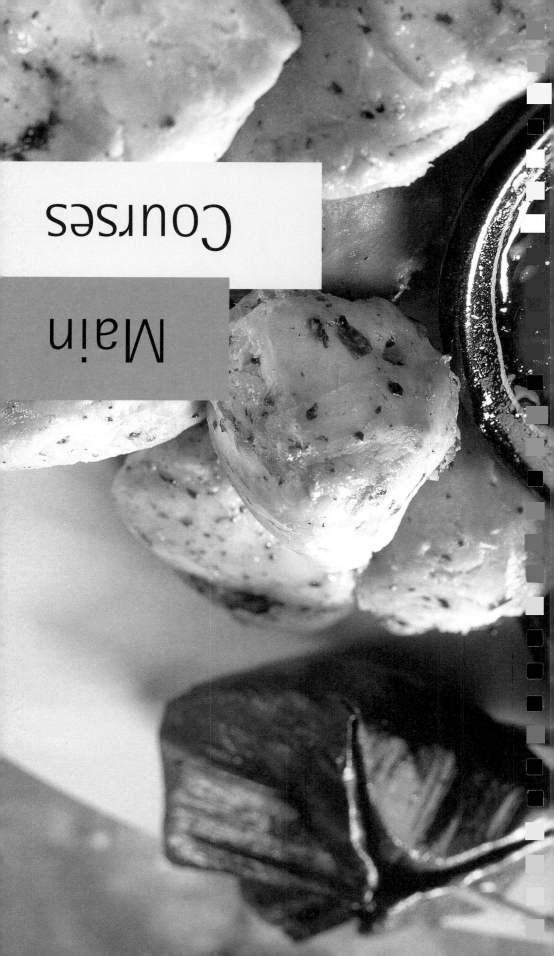

Main
Courses

Grilled Chicken

You need to put in a bit of effort to prepare the chicken, but once marinated it's a tasty candidate for the grill.

serves 4

3 lb 5 oz/1.5 kg whole chicken

grated rind of 1 lemon

4 tbsp lemon juice

2 fresh rosemary sprigs

1 small fresh red chile, finely chopped

⅔ cup olive oil

Method

❶ Split the chicken down the breastbone and open it out. Trim off excess fat, and remove the pope's nose, wing, and leg tips. Break the leg and wing joints to enable you to pound it flat. This ensures that it cooks evenly. Cover the split chicken with plastic wrap and pound it as flat as possible with a rolling pin.

❷ Mix the lemon rind and juice, rosemary sprigs, chile, and olive oil together in a small bowl. Place the chicken in a large dish and pour over the marinade, turning the chicken to coat it evenly. Cover the dish and let the chicken marinate for at least 2 hours in the refrigerator.

❸ Preheat the grill, then cook the chicken over hot coals for about 30 minutes, turning it regularly until the skin is golden and crisp. To test if it is cooked, pierce one of the chicken thighs with a skewer; the juices will run clear, not pink, when it is ready. Serve.

Nutritional Information

Calories	129	Sugars	0g
Protein	22g	Fat	5g
Carbohydrate	0g	Saturates	1g

Chicken Cooked in Banana Leaves

Leaves such as banana are often used in Thai cooking as a natural wrapping for all kinds of ingredients.

serves 4-6

1 garlic clove, chopped

1 tsp finely chopped fresh gingerroot

¼ tsp pepper

2 cilantro sprigs

1 tbsp Thai fish sauce

1 tbsp whiskey

3 skinless, boneless chicken breasts

2–3 banana leaves, cut into

3-inch/7.5-cm squares

corn oil, for pan-frying

chili dipping sauce, to serve

Method

❶ Place the garlic, ginger, pepper, cilantro, fish sauce, and whiskey in a mortar and, using a pestle, grind to a smooth paste.

❷ Cut the chicken into 1-inch/2.5-cm chunks and toss in the paste to coat evenly. Cover and let marinate in the refrigerator for 1 hour.

❸ Place a piece of chicken on a square of banana leaf and wrap it up like a package to enclose the chicken completely. Secure with wooden toothpicks or tie with a piece of string.

❹ Heat a ⅛-inch/3-mm depth of oil in a large, heavy-bottom skillet until hot.

❺ Pan-fry the chicken packages for 8–10 minutes, turning them over occasionally, until golden brown and the chicken is thoroughly cooked. Serve with a chili dipping sauce.

Nutritional Information

Calories	185	Sugars	0g
Protein	18g	Fat	12g
Carbohydrate	0.5g	Saturates	1g

Beef with Wild Mushrooms

Choose fairly thick steaks for this dish to make it easier to cut the pockets.

serves 4

4 sirloin steaks

2 tbsp butter

1–2 garlic cloves, crushed

5½ oz/150 g mixed wild mushrooms, sliced if large

2 tbsp chopped fresh parsley

To serve

salad greens

cherry tomatoes, halved

Method

❶ Preheat the grill. Place the steaks on a cutting board and cut a pocket in the side of each steak.

❷ To make the stuffing, heat the butter in a skillet, then add the garlic and cook gently for about 1 minute.

❸ Add the mushrooms to the skillet and cook gently for 4–6 minutes, or until tender. Stir in the parsley.

❹ Divide the mushroom mixture into 4 and insert a portion into the pocket of each steak. Seal the pocket closed with a toothpick. If preparing ahead, let the mixture cool before stuffing the steaks.

❺ Cook the steaks over hot coals, searing the meat over the hottest part of the grill for about 2 minutes on each side. Move the steaks to an area with slightly less intense heat (usually the sides) and grill for an additional 4–10 minutes on each side, depending on how well done you like your steaks.

❻ Transfer the steaks to serving plates and remove the toothpicks. Serve with salad greens and cherry tomatoes.

Nutritional Information

Calories	414	Sugars	0g
Protein	49g	Fat	24g
Carbohydrate	1g	Saturates	13g

Lamb with Bay & Lemon

Lamb chops are more elegant when the bone is removed to make noisettes.

serves 4

4 lamb chops	⅔ cup lamb or vegetable stock
1 tbsp corn oil	2 bay leaves
1 tbsp butter	pared rind of 1 lemon
⅔ cup white wine	salt and pepper

Method

1 Using a sharp knife, carefully remove the bone from each lamb chop, keeping the meat intact. Alternatively, ask the butcher to prepare the noisettes for you.

2 Shape the meat into circles and secure with a length of string.

3 Heat the oil and butter together in a large skillet until the mixture starts to froth.

4 Add the lamb noisettes to the skillet and cook for 2–3 minutes on each side, or until browned all over.

5 Remove the skillet from the heat and remove the meat, then drain off all of the excess fat and discard. Place the noisettes back in the skillet.

6 Return the skillet to the heat. Add the wine, stock, bay leaves, and lemon rind and cook for 20–25 minutes, or until the lamb is tender. Season the lamb and sauce to taste with a little salt and pepper. Remove and discard the bay leaves.

7 Transfer to serving plates. Remove the string from each noisette and serve with the sauce.

Nutritional Information

Calories	268	Sugars	0.2g
Protein	24g	Fat	16g
Carbohydrate	0.2g	Saturates	7g

Turkey with Cheese Pockets

Wrapping strips of bacon around the turkey helps to enclose the cheese filling.

serves 4

4 turkey breast pieces, about
8 oz/225 g each

salt and pepper

4 portions whole cheese (such as
Bel Paese), ½ oz/15 g each

4 sage leaves or ½ tsp dried sage

8 strips rindless lean bacon

4 tbsp olive oil

2 tbsp lemon juice

To serve

salad greens

cherry tomatoes

Method

❶ Preheat the grill. Carefully cut a pocket into the side of each turkey breast. Open out each breast a little and season inside with salt and pepper.

❷ Place a portion of cheese into each pocket. Tuck a sage leaf into each pocket, or sprinkle with a little dried sage.

❸ Stretch the bacon strips out with the back of a knife. Wrap 2 pieces around each turkey breast, covering the pocket.

❹ Mix the oil and lemon juice together in a small bowl.

❺ Grill the turkey over medium-hot coals, 10 minutes on each side, basting frequently with the lemon mixture.

❻ Transfer the turkey to warmed serving plates. Serve with the salad greens and cherry tomatoes.

Nutritional Information

Calories	518	Sugars	0g
Protein	66g	Fat	28g
Carbohydrate	0g	Saturates	9g

Citrus Duckling Skewers

The tartness of citrus fruit goes well with the rich meat of duckling. Duckling makes a delightful change from chicken for the grill.

serves 12

3 skinless, boneless duckling breasts

1 small red onion, cut into wedges

1 small eggplant, cut into cubes

Marinade

grated rind and juice of 1 lemon

grated rind and juice of 1 lime

grated rind and juice of 1 orange

1 garlic clove, crushed

1 tsp dried oregano

2 tbsp olive oil

dash of Tabasco sauce

Method

❶ Cut the duckling into bite-size pieces. Place in a nonmetallic bowl with the prepared vegetables.

❷ To make the marinade, place the lemon, lime, and orange rinds and juices, garlic, oregano, oil, and Tabasco sauce in a screw-top jar and shake until well combined. Pour the marinade over the duckling and vegetables and toss to coat. Let marinate in the refrigerator for 30 minutes.

❸ Preheat the grill. Remove the duck and vegetables from the marinade and thread them onto presoaked wooden skewers, reserving the marinade.

❹ Grill the skewers on an oiled rack over medium–hot coals, turning and basting frequently with the reserved marinade, for 15–20 minutes, or until the meat is cooked through. Alternatively, cook under a preheated broiler. Serve at once.

Nutritional Information

Calories	205	Sugars	5g
Protein	24g	Fat	10g
Carbohydrate	5g	Saturates	2g

Pork & Sage Kabobs

**The ground pork mixture is shaped into meatballs and threaded onto skewers.
It has a slightly sweet flavor that is popular with children.**

serves 6

1 lb/450 g ground pork

½ cup fresh bread crumbs

1 small onion, very finely chopped

1 tbsp chopped fresh sage

2 tbsp applesauce

¼ tsp ground nutmeg

salt and pepper

Basting mixture

3 tbsp olive oil

1 tbsp lemon juice

To serve

6 small pita breads

mixed salad greens

6 tbsp thick plain yogurt

Method

❶ Place the ground pork in a mixing bowl with the bread crumbs, onion, sage, applesauce, and nutmeg. Season to taste. Mix until the ingredients are combined.

❷ Using your hands, shape the mixture into balls about the size of large marbles. Place on a plate, then cover with plastic wrap and let chill for at least 30 minutes.

❸ Meanwhile, soak 12 small wooden skewers in cold water for at least 30 minutes. Thread the pork meatballs onto the skewers. Cover with plastic wrap and set aside in the refrigerator.

❹ Preheat the grill. To make the baste, combine the olive oil and lemon juice in a small bowl, whisking with a fork until the mixture is well blended.

❺ Grill the kabobs over hot coals for 8–10 minutes, turning and basting frequently with the lemon and oil mixture, until the meat is golden brown and cooked through.

❻ Line the pita breads with the salad greens and spoon over some of the yogurt. Serve with the kabobs.

Nutritional Information

Calories	96	Sugars	0g
Protein	8g	Fat	7g
Carbohydrate	2g	Saturates	2g

Oyster Sauce Lamb

This really is a speedy dish, lamb leg steaks being perfect for
the short cooking time.

serves 4

1 lb/450 g lamb leg steaks	2 tbsp dark soy sauce
1 tsp ground Szechuan pepper	6 tbsp oyster sauce
1 tbsp peanut oil	6 oz/175 g Napa cabbage
2 garlic cloves, crushed	shrimp crackers, to serve (optional)
8 scallions, sliced	

Method

❶ Using a sharp knife, remove any excess fat from the lamb. Slice the lamb thinly.

❷ Sprinkle the ground Szechuan pepper over the meat and toss together until well combined.

❸ Heat the peanut oil in a preheated wok or large, heavy-bottom skillet.

❹ Add the lamb to the wok or skillet and stir-fry for about 5 minutes.

❺ Meanwhile, crush the garlic cloves using a mortar and pestle. Add the garlic and scallions to the wok together with the dark soy sauce and stir-fry for 2 minutes.

❻ Add the oyster sauce and Napa cabbage and stir-fry for an additional 2 minutes, or until the leaves have wilted and the juices are bubbling.

❼ Transfer the stir-fry to warmed serving bowls and serve hot with shrimp crackers, if using.

Cook's tip

Oyster sauce is made from oysters, which are cooked in brine and soy sauce. Sold in bottles, it will keep in the refrigerator for months.

Nutritional Information

Calories	243	Sugars	0.4g
Protein	26g	Fat	14g
Carbohydrate	3g	Saturates	5g

Grilled Herrings with Lemon

Cooking these fish in foil packages gives them a wonderfully moist texture.

serves 4

4 herrings, cleaned and scaled

4 bay leaves

salt

1 lemon, sliced

4 tbsp unsalted butter

2 tbsp chopped fresh parsley

½ tsp lemon pepper

fresh crusty bread, to serve

Method

❶ Preheat the grill. Season the prepared herrings inside and out with salt to taste.

❷ Place a bay leaf inside the cavity of each fish.

❸ Place 4 squares of foil on the counter and divide the lemon slices evenly between them. Place a fish on top of the lemon slices on each of the foil squares.

❹ Beat the butter until softened, then mix in the parsley and lemon pepper. Dot the flavored butter liberally over the fish.

❺ Wrap the fish tightly in the foil and grill over medium–hot coals for 15–20 minutes, or until the fish is cooked through—the flesh should be white in color and firm to the touch (unwrap the foil to check, then rewrap).

❻ Transfer the wrapped fish packages to warmed serving plates.

❼ Unwrap the foil packages just before serving and serve the fish with fresh crusty bread to mop up the deliciously flavored cooking juices.

Nutritional Information

Calories	355	Sugars	0g
Protein	19g	Fat	31g
Carbohydrate	0g	Saturates	13g

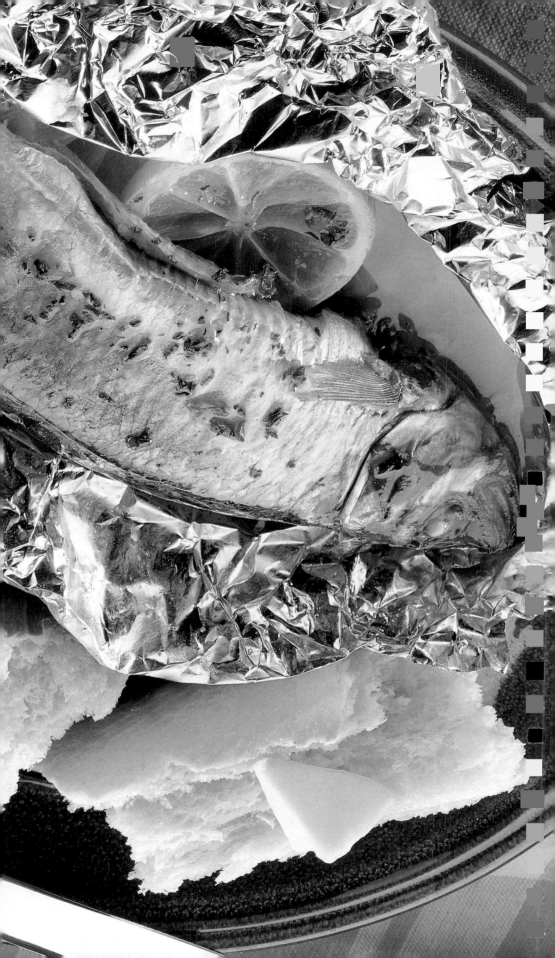

Marinated Fish

Marinating fish, for even a short time, adds a subtle flavor to the flesh and makes even simply broiled or cooked fish delicious.

serves 4

4 whole trout or mackerel, cleaned

4 tbsp chopped fresh marjoram

2 tbsp extra virgin olive oil

finely grated rind and juice of 1 lime

2 garlic cloves, crushed

salt and pepper

lime wedges, to garnish

salad greens, to serve

Method

❶ Using a sharp knife, cut 4 or 5 diagonal slashes on each side of the fish. Place the fish in a shallow, nonmetallic dish.

❷ To make the marinade, mix together the marjoram, olive oil, lime rind and juice, garlic, and salt and pepper in a bowl.

❸ Pour the mixture over the fish. Let marinate in the refrigerator for about 30 minutes.

❹ Preheat the broiler. Cook the fish under the hot broiler for 5–6 minutes on each side, brushing occasionally with the reserved marinade, until golden.

❺ Transfer the fish to serving plates. Pour over any remaining marinade before serving, garnished with lime wedges and salad greens.

Cook's tip

If the lime is too hard to squeeze, microwave on high power for 30 seconds to release the juice. This dish is also excellent cooked on the grill.

Nutritional Information

Calories	361	Sugars	0g
Protein	26g	Fat	29g
Carbohydrate	0g	Saturates	5g

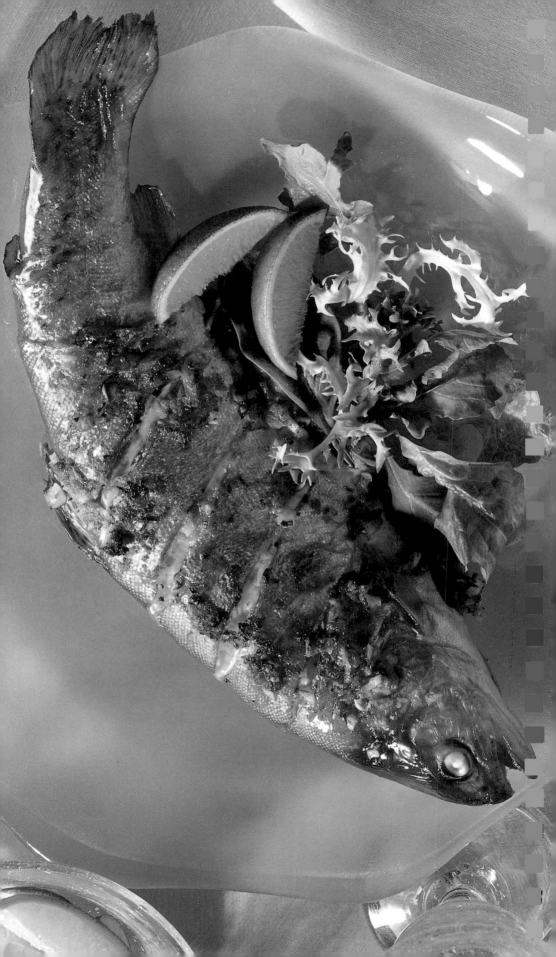

Gingered Angler Fish

This dish is a real treat and is perfect for special occasions. Angler fish
has a tender flavor, which is ideal with asparagus, chili sauce, and ginger.

serves 4

1 lb/450 g angler fish

1 tbsp grated fresh gingerroot

2 tbsp sweet chili sauce

1 tbsp corn oil

3½ oz/100 g fine asparagus

3 scallions, diagonally sliced

1 tsp sesame oil

Method

❶ Cut the angler fish into bite-size pieces.
Mix the ginger and chili sauce together in
a bowl until thoroughly blended. Using a
pastry brush, brush the ginger and chili
sauce mixture over the angler fish pieces.

❷ Heat the corn oil in a preheated wok or
large, heavy-bottom skillet.

❸ Add the angler fish, asparagus, and
scallions to the wok and stir-fry
for 5 minutes, stirring gently so the fish
pieces and asparagus do not break up.

❹ Remove the wok from the heat, then
drizzle the sesame oil over the stir-fry and
toss well to combine.

❺ Transfer the angler fish to warmed
serving plates and serve at once.

Cook's tip

*Angler fish is quite expensive, but it is well worth
using as it has a wonderful flavor and texture. You
could use cubes of chunky cod fillet instead.*

Nutritional Information

Calories	133	Sugars	0g
Protein	21g	Fat	5g
Carbohydrate	1g	Saturates	1g

Thai Spiced Salmon

Marinated in delicate Thai spices and quickly pan-fried to perfection,
these salmon fillets are ideal for a special dinner. Serve them fresh from
the skillet to enjoy them at their best.

serves 4

1-inch/2.5-cm piece fresh
gingerroot, grated

1 tsp coriander seeds, crushed

¼ tsp chili powder

1 tbsp lime juice

1 tsp sesame oil

4 salmon fillet pieces with skin,
about 5½ oz/150 g each

2 tbsp vegetable oil

cilantro leaves, to garnish

To serve

stir-fried vegetables

freshly cooked rice

Method

❶ Mix the ginger, crushed coriander, chili powder, lime juice, and sesame oil together in a bowl.

❷ Place the salmon on a wide, nonmetallic plate or dish and spoon the mixture over the flesh side of the fillets, spreading it to coat each piece of salmon evenly.

❸ Cover the dish with plastic wrap and let chill in the refrigerator for 30 minutes.

❹ Heat a wide, heavy-bottom skillet or ridged grill pan with the vegetable oil over high heat. Place the salmon in the hot skillet, skin-side down, and cook for 4–5 minutes, without turning, until the salmon is crusty underneath and the flesh flakes easily.

❺ Serve immediately, with stir-fried vegetables and freshly cooked rice, garnished with cilantro leaves.

Nutritional Information

Calories	329	Sugars	0g
Protein	30g	Fat	23g
Carbohydrate	0g	Saturates	4g

Fragrant Tuna Steaks

Fresh tuna steaks are very meaty—they have a firm texture, yet the flesh is succulent. Tuna is rich in valuable omega 3 oils.

serves 4

4 tuna steaks, about 6 oz/175 g each

½ tsp finely grated lime rind

1 garlic clove, crushed

2 tsp olive oil

1 tsp ground cumin

1 tsp ground coriander

pepper

1 tbsp lime juice

cilantro, to garnish

To serve

avocado relish (see Cook's Tip)

tomato wedges

lime wedges

Method

❶ Trim the skin from the tuna steaks and rinse under cold running water, then pat dry on paper towels.

❷ Mix the grated lime rind, garlic, olive oil, cumin, ground coriander, and pepper to taste, together in a small bowl to form a paste.

❸ Spread the paste thinly on both sides of the tuna. Heat a nonstick, ridged grill pan until hot and press the tuna steaks into the pan to seal them. Reduce the heat and cook for 5 minutes. Turn the fish over and cook for an additional 4–5 minutes, or until the fish is cooked through. Drain on paper towels and transfer to a warmed serving plate.

❹ Sprinkle the lime juice and cilantro over the fish. Serve at once with avocado relish, and tomato and lime wedges.

Cook's tip

For the avocado relish, peel, pit, and chop a small ripe avocado. Mix in 1 tablespoon lime juice, 1 tablespoon chopped cilantro, 1 finely chopped small red onion, and some chopped mango or tomato. Season to taste.

Nutritional Information

Calories	239	Sugars	0.1g
Protein	42g	Fat	8g
Carbohydrate	0.5g	Saturates	2g

Butterfly Shrimp

These shrimp look stunning when presented on the skewers, and they will certainly impress as part of a main meal.

serves 2-4

1 lb 2 oz/500 g or 16 raw jumbo shrimp, shelled, leaving tails intact

juice of 2 limes

1 tsp cardamom seeds

2 tsp cumin seeds, ground

2 tsp coriander seeds, ground

½ tsp ground cinnamon

1 tsp ground turmeric

1 garlic clove, crushed

1 tsp cayenne pepper

2 tbsp oil

cucumber slices, to garnish

Method

❶ Soak 8 wooden skewers in water for 20 minutes. Cut the shrimp lengthwise in half down to the tail and flatten out to form a symmetrical shape.

❷ Thread a shrimp onto 2 wooden skewers, with the tail between them, so that, when laid flat, the skewers hold the shrimp in shape. Thread another 3 shrimp onto these 2 skewers in the same way. Repeat until you have 4 sets of 4 shrimp each.

❸ Lay the skewered shrimp in a nonporous, nonmetallic dish, and sprinkle over the lime juice.

❹ Combine the spices and the oil, and coat the shrimp well in the mixture. Cover the shrimp and let chill for 4 hours.

❺ Preheat the grill or broiler. Cook the shrimp over hot coals or under the hot broiler for 6 minutes, turning once.

❻ Serve at once, garnished with the cucumber slices and accompanied by yogurt or a sweet chutney—walnut chutney is ideal.

Nutritional Information

Calories	183	Sugars	0g
Protein	28g	Fat	8g
Carbohydrate	0g	Saturates	1g

Scallops with Mushrooms

Scallops have a rich but delicate flavor. When sautéed with mushrooms and bathed in brandy and cream, they make a really special meal.

serves 2

1 tbsp butter

8 oz/225 g shelled scallops

1 tbsp olive oil

scant 1 cup sliced oyster mushrooms

scant 1 cup sliced shiitake mushrooms

1 garlic clove, chopped

4 scallions, white and green parts sliced

3 tbsp heavy cream

1 tbsp brandy

salt and pepper

fresh dill sprigs, to garnish

freshly cooked basmati rice, to serve

Method

❶ Heat the butter in a heavy-bottom skillet and sauté the scallops for about 1 minute, turning occasionally.

❷ Remove the scallops from the skillet with a slotted spoon and keep warm.

❸ Add the oil to the skillet and heat. Add the mushrooms, garlic, and scallions and cook for 2 minutes, stirring constantly.

❹ Return the scallops to the skillet. Add the heavy cream and brandy, stirring well to mix.

❺ Season to taste with salt and pepper and heat to warm through. Garnish with fresh dill sprigs and serve with rice.

Nutritional Information

Calories	350	Sugars	1g
Protein	31g	Fat	28g
Carbohydrate	1g	Saturates	4g

Spinach Frittata

A frittata is another word for a large, thick omelet. This is an Italian dish,
which may be made with many flavorings. Spinach is used as the main
ingredient in this recipe for color and flavor.

serves 4

1 lb/450 g fresh spinach leaves

2 tsp water

4 eggs, beaten

2 tbsp light cream

2 garlic cloves, crushed

1¾ oz/50 g canned corn kernels, drained

1 celery stalk, chopped

1 fresh red chile, chopped

2 tomatoes, seeded and diced

2 tbsp olive oil

2 tbsp butter

¼ cup pecan halves

2 tbsp grated romano cheese

1 oz/25 g fontina cheese, cubed

pinch of paprika

Method

❶ Cook the spinach in the water in a
covered pan for 5 minutes. Drain
thoroughly and pat dry on paper towels.

❷ Beat the eggs in a bowl and stir in the
spinach, cream, garlic, corn, celery, chile,
and tomatoes. Mix well.

❸ Heat the oil and butter in an
8-inch/20-cm heavy-bottom skillet.

❹ Spoon the egg mixture into the skillet
and sprinkle with the pecan halves,
romano and fontina cheeses, and paprika.
Cook, without stirring, over medium heat
for 5–7 minutes, or until the underside of
the frittata is brown.

❺ Place a large plate over the skillet and
invert to turn out the frittata. Slide it back
into the skillet and cook the other side for
an additional 2–3 minutes. Serve the
frittata straight from the skillet.
Alternatively, transfer to a serving plate.

Nutritional Information

Calories 307		Sugars 4g	
Protein 15g		Fat 25g	
Carbohydrate 6g		Saturates 8g	

Eggplant Rolls

Thin slices of eggplant are cooked in olive oil and garlic, and then topped with pesto sauce and finely sliced mozzarella.

serves 4

2 eggplants, thinly sliced lengthwise	6 oz/175 g mozzarella cheese, grated
5 tbsp olive oil	fresh basil leaves, torn into pieces
1 garlic clove, crushed	salt and pepper
4 tbsp pesto	fresh basil leaves, to garnish

Method

❶ Preheat the oven to 350°F/180°C. Sprinkle the eggplant slices liberally with salt and leave for 10–15 minutes to extract the bitter juices. Turn the slices over and repeat. Rinse with cold water and drain on paper towels.

❷ Heat the olive oil in a large skillet and add the garlic and eggplant slices, a few at a time. Cook the eggplant lightly on both sides. Remove with a slotted spoon and drain them on paper towels.

❸ Spread a little pesto onto one side of each of the eggplant slices. Top with the mozzarella and sprinkle with basil leaves. Season with a little salt and pepper. Roll up and secure with toothpicks.

❹ Arrange the eggplant rolls in a greased ovenproof baking dish. Place in the preheated oven and bake for 8–10 minutes.

❺ Transfer the eggplant rolls to a warmed serving plate. Sprinkle with fresh basil leaves and serve at once.

Cook's tip

You could use sliced zucchini instead of the eggplant. They will take less time to cook.

Nutritional Information

Calories	278	Sugars	2g
Protein	4g	Fat	28g
Carbohydrate	2g	Saturates	7g

Ma-Po Tofu

Ma-Po was the wife of a Szechuan chef who created this popular dish in the middle of the 19th century.

serves 4

3 packages tofu, about 8 oz/225 g each

3 tbsp vegetable oil

generous ½ cup coarsely ground beef

½ tsp finely chopped garlic

1 leek, cut into short sections

½ tsp salt

1 tbsp black bean sauce

1 tbsp light soy sauce

1 tsp chili bean sauce

3–4 tbsp chicken or vegetable stock

2 tsp cornstarch

3 tsp cold water

few drops sesame oil

pepper

finely chopped scallions,
to garnish

Method

❶ Drain the tofu and cut into ½-inch/1-cm cubes, handling it carefully.

❷ Bring some water to a boil in a small pan or wok, then add the tofu and blanch for 2–3 minutes to harden. Remove and drain well.

❸ Heat the oil in a preheated wok. Add the ground beef and garlic and stir-fry for about 1 minute, or until the color of the beef changes. Add the leek, salt, and sauces and blend well.

❹ Add the stock followed by the tofu. Bring to a boil and braise gently for 2–3 minutes.

❺ Mix the cornstarch with the water until it forms a smooth paste, then add to the wok and stir until the sauce has thickened. Sprinkle with sesame oil and pepper, then garnish with scallions. Serve hot.

Cook's tip

Tofu has been an important element in Chinese cooking for more than 1000 years. Tofu is highly nutritious, being rich in protein and low in fat.

Nutritional Information

Calories	235	Sugars	1g
Protein	16g	Fat	18g
Carbohydrate	3g	Saturates	4g

Desserts

Coconut Candy

Quick and easy to make, this candy is very similar to coconut ice. Pink food coloring may be added toward the end if desired.

serves 4-6

scant ¾ cup butter

1½ cups dry unsweetened coconut

¾ cup sweetened condensed milk

few drops pink food coloring (optional)

Method

❶ Place the butter in a heavy-bottom pan and melt over low heat, stirring.

❷ Add the dry unsweetened coconut to the melted butter, stirring to mix.

❸ Stir in the condensed milk and the pink food coloring, if using, and mix for an additional 7–10 minutes, stirring constantly.

❹ Remove the pan from the heat, then set aside and let the coconut mixture cool slightly.

❺ Once cool enough to handle, shape the coconut mixture into long blocks, and cut into equal-size rectangles. Let stand for about 1 hour, until set, then serve.

Cook's tip

Coconut is used extensively in Indian cooking to add flavor and creaminess to various dishes. The best flavor comes from freshly grated coconut, although ready-prepared dry unsweetened coconut, as used here, makes an excellent standby. Freshly grated coconut freezes well, so it is worth preparing when you have the time.

Nutritional Information

Calories	338	Sugars	5g
Protein	4g	Fat	34g
Carbohydrate	5g	Saturates	26g

Italian Chocolate Truffles

These are flavored with almonds and chocolate, and are simplicity itself to make.
Served with coffee, they are the perfect end to a meal.

makes 24

6 squares semisweet chocolate

2 tbsp almond-flavored liqueur or

orange-flavored liqueur

3 tbsp unsalted butter

scant ½ cup confectioners' sugar

½ cup ground almonds

1¾ squares milk chocolate, grated

Method

❶ Melt the semisweet chocolate with the liqueur in a bowl set over a pan of hot water, stirring until well combined.

❷ Add the butter and stir until it has melted. Stir in the confectioners' sugar and the ground almonds.

❸ Let the mixture stand in a cool place until firm enough to roll into 24 balls.

❹ Place the grated milk chocolate on a plate and roll the truffles in the chocolate to coat them.

❺ Place the truffles in paper candy cases and let chill.

Variation

Almond-flavored liqueur gives these truffles an authentic Italian flavor. The original almond liqueur, Amaretto di Saronno, comes from Saronno in Italy.

Nutritional Information

Calories	82	Sugars	7g
Protein	1g	Fat	5g
Carbohydrate	8g	Saturates	3g

Italian-Style Strawberries

Generations of Italian cooks have known that the unlikely combination of freshly ground black pepper and ripe, juicy strawberries is fantastic.

serves 4-6

1 lb/450 g fresh strawberries

2–3 tbsp balsamic vinegar

pepper

fresh mint leaves, torn, plus extra to decorate (optional)

½–¾ cup mascarpone cheese

Method

❶ Wipe the strawberries with a damp cloth, rather than rinsing them, so they do not become soggy. Using a paring knife, cut off the green stems at the top and use the tip of the knife to remove the core or hull.

❷ Cut each hulled strawberry in half lengthwise or into fourths if large. Transfer to a bowl.

❸ Add the balsamic vinegar, allowing ½ tablespoon per person. Add several twists of ground black pepper, then gently stir together. Cover with plastic wrap and let chill for up to 4 hours.

❹ Just before serving, stir in torn fresh mint leaves to taste. Spoon the mascarpone into bowls and spoon the strawberries on top. Decorate with a few mint leaves, if desired. Sprinkle with extra pepper to taste.

Cook's tip

This is most enjoyable when it is made with the best-quality balsamic vinegar, one that has aged slowly and has turned thick and syrupy. Unfortunately, the genuine mixture is always expensive. Less expensive versions are artificially sweetened and colored with caramel.

Nutritional Information

Calories	132	Sugars	5g
Protein	1g	Fat	12g
Carbohydrate	5g	Saturates	7g

Mocha Swirl Mousse

A featherlight yet richly moreish combination, these chocolate and coffee mousses
are attractively presented in tall glasses.

serves 4

1 tbsp coffee and chicory extract

2 tsp unsweetened cocoa,
plus extra for dusting

1 tsp lowfat drinking chocolate powder

⅔ cup lowfat sour cream,
plus 4 tsp to serve

2 tsp powdered gelozone

2 tbsp boiling water

2 large egg whites

2 tbsp superfine sugar

4 chocolate coffee beans, to serve

Method

❶ Place the coffee and chicory extract
in a bowl, and the cocoa and drinking
chocolate in a second bowl. Divide the
sour cream between the 2 bowls and
mix both well.

❷ Dissolve the gelozone in the boiling
water and set aside. In a greasefree
bowl, whisk the egg whites and sugar
until stiff, then divide this evenly between
the 2 mixtures.

❸ Divide the dissolved gelozone between
the 2 mixtures and, using a large metal
spoon, gently fold until well mixed.

❹ Spoon small amounts of the 2 mousses
alternately into 4 serving glasses and swirl
together gently. Place in the refrigerator
and let chill for about 1 hour, or until set.

❺ To serve, top each mousse with a
teaspoonful of sour cream, a chocolate
coffee bean, and a light dusting of cocoa.
Serve at once.

Cook's tip

*Gelozone, the vegetarian equivalent of gelatin,
is available from most health food stores.*

Nutritional Information

Calories	136	Sugars	10g
Protein	5g	Fat	8g
Carbohydrate	11g	Saturates	5g

Lemon Jumbles

These lemony, melt-in-the-mouth cookies are made extra special by dredging with confectioners' sugar just before serving.

makes 50

scant ½ cup butter, softened, plus extra for greasing

scant ¾ cup superfine sugar

grated rind of 1 lemon

1 egg, beaten

4 tbsp lemon juice

2¼ cups all-purpose flour, plus extra for dusting

1 tsp baking powder

1 tbsp milk

confectioners' sugar, for dredging

Method

❶ Preheat the oven to 325°F/160°C, then lightly grease several baking sheets. Beat the butter, superfine sugar, and lemon rind together in a large bowl until pale and fluffy. Add the beaten egg and lemon juice, a little at a time, beating well after each addition.

❷ Sift the flour and baking powder into the creamed mixture and blend together. Add the milk, mixing to form a soft dough.

❸ Turn the dough out onto a lightly floured counter and divide into 50 equal-size pieces.

❹ Roll each piece into a sausage shape with your hands and twist in the middle to make an "S" shape. Place the shapes on the baking sheets and bake in the oven for 15–20 minutes. Transfer to a wire rack and let cool completely. Dredge with confectioners' sugar to serve.

Nutritional Information

Calories	50	Sugars	3g
Protein	1g	Fat	2g
Carbohydrate	8g	Saturates	1g

Exotic Fruit Packages

Tempting pieces of exotic fruit are warmed through in a deliciously scented sauce to make a fabulous grill dessert.

serves 4

1 papaya	3 tbsp orange juice
1 mango	light cream or lowfat plain yogurt,
1 carambola	to serve
1 tbsp grenadine	

Method

1 Cut the papaya in half, then scoop out the seeds and discard them. Peel the papaya and cut the flesh into thick slices.

2 Prepare the mango by cutting it in half lengthwise and carefully cutting the flesh away from the flat central pit.

3 Score each mango half in a criss-cross pattern. Push each half inside out to separate the cubes and cut them away from the peel.

4 Using a sharp knife, thickly slice the carambola.

5 Place all of the fruit in a bowl and mix them together. Mix the grenadine and orange juice together and pour over the fruit. Let marinate for at least 30 minutes.

6 Preheat the grill. Divide the fruit between 4 double thickness squares of foil and gather up the edges to form a package that encloses the fruit. Place the foil package on a rack set over warm coals and grill the fruit for 15–20 minutes.

7 Serve the fruit in the package, with the lowfat plain yogurt.

Nutritional Information

Calories	43	Sugars	9g
Protein	2g	Fat	0.3g
Carbohydrate	9g	Saturates	0.1g

Rose Ice

This is a delicately perfumed sweet granita ice. It looks very pretty piled on a glass dish with rose petals sprinkled over.

serves 4

1¾ cups water

2 tbsp coconut cream

4 tbsp sweetened condensed milk

2 tsp rose water

few drops pink food coloring (optional)

pink rose petals, to decorate

Method

❶ Place the water in a small pan and add the coconut cream. Heat the mixture gently without boiling, stirring constantly.

❷ Remove the pan from the heat and let cool. Stir in the condensed milk, rose water, and food coloring, if using.

❸ Pour the mixture into a large, freezerproof container and freeze for 1–1½ hours, or until slushy.

❹ Remove from the freezer and break up the ice crystals with a fork. Return to the freezer and freeze until firm.

❺ Spoon the ice roughly into a pile on a serving dish and sprinkle with rose petals to serve.

Cook's tip

To prevent the ice thawing too quickly at the table, nestle the base of the serving dish in another dish filled with crushed ice.

Nutritional Information

Calories	76	Sugars	9g
Protein	2g	Fat	4g
Carbohydrate	9g	Saturates	3g

Recipe List

- Avocado Cream Terrine *24* • Beef with Wild Mushrooms *48*

- Butterfly Shrimp *70* • Chicken Cooked in Banana Leaves *46* • Chicory Salad *40*

- Chile & Watercress Soup *12* • Chinese Crab Soup *16* • Citrus Duckling Skewers *54*

- Coconut Candy *82* • Cream of Chicken Soup *10* • Easy Cauliflower & Broccoli *28*

- Eggplant Rolls *76* • Eggplant Satay *22* • Exotic Fruit Packages *92*

- Fragrant Tuna Steaks *68* • Gingered Angler Fish *64* • Grilled Chicken *44*

- Grilled Herrings with Lemon *60* • Green Sesame Salad *38*

- Grilled Smoked Salmon *18* • Italian Chocolate Truffles *84*

- Italian-Style Strawberries *86* • Lamb with Bay & Lemon *50* • Lemon Jumbles *90*

- Lettuce-Wrapped Meat *20* • Lobster Salad *36* • Long Beans with Tomatoes *32*

- Ma-Po Tofu *78* • Marinated Fish *62* • Mixed Leaf Salad *34*

- Mocha Swirl Mousse *88* • Oyster Sauce Lamb *58* • Pork & Sage Kabobs *56*

- Roasted Vegetables *30* • Rose Ice *94* • Scallops with Mushrooms *72*

- Spinach & Ginger Soup *14* • Spinach Frittata *74* • Thai Spiced Salmon *66*

- Thai Stuffed Omelet *26* • Turkey with Cheese Pockets *52*